Establishing a Culture of

# Lead Worshipers
## How to Build a Worship Team

STEPHEN ROBERT CASS

PHOENIX, AZ

An imprint of Solid Walnut Music
15620S. 14th Place
Phoenix, AZ  85048
songs4god.net

Send feedback to feedback@songs4god.net

Copyright© 2014, 2021 by Stephen Robert Cass
All rights reserved by Solid Walnut Music,
who believes in sanctity of copyright. It fuels creativity
and diversity, promotes free speech,
and helps our culture flourish.

Thank you for buying an authorized version of this book,
and for not distributing, copying, or reproducing it in any manner
without written permission (except for brief quotes).
You are supporting Solid Walnut Music to continue to publish books the reader wants.

Printed in the United States of America

10 9 8 7 6 5 4 3 2

Library of Congress Cataloging-in-Publication Data
Cass, Stephen Robert
establishing a culture of
lead worshipers
how to build a worship team
by Stephen Robert Cass.
1. Cass, Stephen Robert—Religion 2. leadership

ISBN  978-1-7378891-1-3 (pdf)
ISBN  978-1-7378891-2-0 (epub, ASIN)
ISBN  978-1-7378891-0-6 (pbk)
ISBN  978-8-9855371-0-9 (audio)

Scriptures taken from the
HOLY BIBLE, NEW INTERNATIONAL VERSION,
Copyright © 1973,1978, 1984
by International Bible Society.
Used by permission of Zondervan Publishing House.

All graphics in this book are the sole property of Solid Walnut Music,
who reserves all rights. Reproductions for commentary uses are permitted
with acknowledgement to Song4God.net Media and Stephen Robert Cass.
Any reproduction for the purpose of commerce must have written permission.

Cover design: Songs4God.net Media
Printing in the Unites States: IngramSpark and Amazon KDP

Significant discounts for bulk print
and e-book sales are available
by emailing steve@songs4god.net
or call (480) 773-3484

2nd Edition: new publisher and Prelude update

*Prelude*

## For One Reason Only

We worship for one reason only: to give thanks for what God has done for us. We gather to learn how we can recognize the power of the full-time gift of the Holy Spirit. That's the deal that Jesus made with us: He goes, or the Spirit, The Advocate, will not come. See John 16:7.

That's pretty easy to understand. Marching orders, I call it: "I'm going for a reason, something better is coming." And that's why we do what we do in a church that follows Jesus. Oh, but we try and do different stuff, like argue over carpet color, because, hey, we're all flawed. But the reason for worship is cut and dried.

*Everyone on the platform is a lead worshiper.* The face of your church. With 50 years of experience as a worship team member and leader, songwriter, and church planter, I bring you my blueprint of how a music ministry will blossom on a solid foundation.

As leaders of the worship service, we have a job: to build a team of heartfelt Jesus followers to stand up front. In this book, read about team building strategies to ...

- Promote sacrifice for the sake of the team and the mission of the church
- Show invitation to the foot of the cross in all faces on the platform
- Amplify the heart of worship in each member

- Create solid ideas, such as a worship choir on the platform with the band
- Remove distractions from the platform

No doubt, there are many different viewpoints on how 'church' should be done. There are conservative and progressive and orthodox and every model in between. There are European, American, Australian, African and Asian ways of thinking on how to form a church. Even when there is a basic understanding, there are different thoughts on growth models and whether or not to be inclusive of seekers, and questions about baptism, etc. etc. etc.

What to think! Well, Jesus Christ established this church on earth through Peter and the Disciples and said the gates of hell would not prevail against it. There is a viewpoint that says that God, and only God, should go forth and to continue to build churches on earth. But I contend that we as the hands and feet of Christ are to partner with God in building our earthly churches, following the model of the words of Jesus and the early church formation in the Book of Acts. The veil is torn and we can call upon the Holy of Holies!

The Bible is very clear in many passages about how our free will is a fact in our existence and that we will take this into account with our actions. Proverbs 3:5-6 tell us to 'lean not on our own understanding'.

> Trust in the LORD with all **your** heart and **lean not on your own understanding**; in all **your** ways submit to him, and he will make **your** paths straight.

Many verses like this one remind us that God gave us the brains to figure out how to navigate life. But the verse also gives us the important message about the balance in our thinking: 'trust in the LORD with all your heart'. The combination of these two thoughts is the key! This tells us that we had better consult with God and not be so taken with our own viewpoints. See how James chapter 4 captures this line of thinking as well.

So, let us not be so taken with our own viewpoints as we build our churches, but let us lean on the wisdom of God. Let us then build the culture of worship within our churches so we don't build services to be a monument of a man or woman. Let us not worship a church service. Let us build our worship culture around the true meaning of worship and around the service of the people who come to celebrate the living God every Sunday and throughout the week!

Let every question on how we build our worship, whether it's the decisions on lighting or the selection of the songs, revolve around helping people worship. Let us learn the importance of understanding why people come to church and what they expect to experience. And finally, but of primary importance: Let us remove anything that is a distraction from these goals. Let us return to the heart of worship.

Building a worship culture is a set of tasks that require time on the knees. We're talking about dealing with human beings with all kinds of thoughts and ways of dealing with life as we try and balance that with what God has given us as a vision. All of this rides on the teeter-totter of discerning the true nature of worship balanced with my tendency to cause pain in life, if only because of my tendency to do what I do not want to do (read and study Romans chapter 7).

This book is primarily written about establishing a culture of lead worshipers for the platform and for the technical crew, no matter the affiliation or form of church. This book is *not* about how a planting pastor, the planting worship leader and other leadership view detailed aspects of building a church.

I truly believe that the basis for worship is found within the words of Jesus in his conversation with the woman at Jacob's well in Samaria, found in John chapter 4.

**21 "Woman," Jesus replied, "believe me, a time is coming when you will worship the Father neither on this mountain nor in Jerusalem. 22 You Samaritans worship what you do not know; we worship what we**

**do know, for salvation is from the Jews. 23 Yet a time is coming and has now come when the true worshipers will worship the Father in the Spirit and in truth, for they are the kind of worshipers the Father seeks. 24 God is spirit, and his worshipers must worship in the Spirit and in truth."**

Taken in the entire context, Chapter 4 sets the backdrop for this conversation very well and is worth the time to study. This is where the bottom-line description of worship is told to us. I expand more on this bottom line as it relates to our attitudes during worship in the section entitled *What to Bring to the Platform*.

Take these building blocks to into your heart and fit them as you see them working together. See how these can work for you and help you worship, whether you are in the worship band, choir or are a church planter or worship leader.

I am alive for sake of Christ!

# CONTENTS

## Chapter 1: | Phase Overview
Phase 1: Excellence
Phase 2 and 3 Overview
Phase 2: Color

## Chapter 2: | Phase 3: Community
The Expansion of the Music Ministry
Hold Regular Auditions
Establish Two Choirs
Establish a Songwriting Ministry
Nights of Worship
Offer Worship Music to Ministries

## Chapter 3: | Excellence in Worship
Attitudes and Focus
We Encourage Others to Worship
Removing Distractions
We Must Raise the Bar
We Live and Worship in God's Economy
The Call of Sacrifice
My Service Pledge

## Chapter 4: | Connecting in Worship
To Be Captured and Engaged
To Experience Moments
To Be Transformed
Our Sacrifice
Excusing Yourself from the Team
Leadership in Worship

## Chapter 5: | Worship Expressions

## Chapter 6: | What to Bring to the Platform

About the Author
Titles by Stephen Robert Cass

# Chapter 1:
# Phase Overview

This is a 10,000 ft. view of how a worship culture could be established. It tells the basic story of how church planters might view the evolution of the culture and what pieces might come in to play along the way. The beautiful part is that this is only my vision, and others will have marvelous success mixing and matching other components. And I'm positive that I've never thought of many wonderful ways to build a system that have worked well for others. God is good and always the bottom line; Jesus is Lord and always the Centerpiece.

> *A note about the Phases and this book: all Phases could happen simultaneously, but some may find that they would like to go one Phase at a time. Overall, there is nothing more important than Phase 1. So, this book is all about Phase 1 with brief overviews of Phases 2 and 3.*

# LEAD WORSHIPERS

*The next section in this book, Excellence in Worship, is the beginning point for a 'worship team manual', a manual that can describe how each member can participate.*

*Just as building faith with the strong foundation of Christ is a biblical model, so is building worship on the strong platform of washing the feet of your congregation as outlined in Phase 1. The key is to serve them, not ourselves. I would never advocate philosophies or suggest anything would be of a self-indulgent nature! Selfishness can be cancerous to the worship experience.*

## Phase 1: Excellence

### Notes on the 80/20 and 110% Rules

*Please note*: I am going to refer to "giving 110% to Jesus" in this book in regard to building and maintaining a worship team. The reality in serving churches is often the 80/20 rule, where 80% of the work is done by 20% of the people. Many churches will always exist with this ratio, even after they become larger.

In the section on Excellence and even beyond in this book, I call for the musician/worshiper to have a heart of dedicating 110% to the team in musical and spiritual preparedness, as well as during song time. The reality of many music ministries is that several people serving there may also be taking care of other church ministries and jobs. The call for 110% dedication might be a perfect fit for a larger church, where the musicians are ONLY musicians, and the

## PHASE OVERVIEW

call for 110% might seem overbearing for a smaller church.

I would like to argue that the 110% rule remain as the goal for the worship team. Let the lead worshiper decide how.

It's important to continually give the band and technicians the visions of the church. One of these visions should be the hope that the 80/20 rule will pass, not only for the music but for all ministries. I believe that discussion and prayer should be around why the 80/20 rule might be a reality, but should not be the norm. This is a very worthy item to include on the prayer chain. But let's stick with the music ministry for our purpose, and let me explain why I believe that the leaders of this ministry strive toward the 110% rule. We should make this a part of the music worship ministry DNA from day one for one very good reason!

*The reason: The music and worship ministry are the face of your church.* We are called to be visible, and we should embrace that. I'm not saying, at all, that the coffee and children's ministries are secondary or somehow less important. What I am saying is that the worship atmosphere and music is at the top of the list of scrutiny when people come and visit your church. This might be the very main reason why they will or will not come back next Sunday.

A great worship atmosphere demands that everyone who is on the platform be approachable. Everyone on the platform should show the face of the 110% rule in order to give the message that they are there to serve, and to serve with no distractions and with focus.

A very important part of this equation is that people are given the chance to rest. Regular time away should be scheduled for people. There is more information on the 110% rule in the next section.

A second reason for embracing 110% is that when and if your church becomes larger, leadership might be ready for the reality past 80/20. There will be more and more musicians who will compete for your time, and leadership should be ready to maintain a team that is strong with purpose of worship and music.

It's important to me as a lead worshiper to model the 110% rule in order to lead others toward its noble goals.

Let's Get Started!

Musicians, hopefully home-grown and dedicated members of the new church, are volunteers or are identified. I only say 'hopefully' because my vision includes unity of the serving body; one team and one goal. Having outside musicians who may or may not be members of the church or followers of Christ might present a challenge in having initial unity. But God will work in His way and with whomever He chooses!

There will be those who wish to have worship services using traditional music. Categories of music will forever be a moving target as 'traditional' can either mean hymns from 19th and 20th century, Gaither band material, or it can mean the praise and worship 'revolution' of Maranatha! in the 1970's. A blended service might mean that the music planned might be a mix of traditional and more current worship titles. Regardless of categories or styles, Jesus tells us in John 4:24 that God desires people who want to worship Him in spirit and in truth. Let us continually ask ourselves how to do this!

# PHASE OVERVIEW

Regardless of the music chosen, let us utilize the songs as tools to worship the living God. There is always the opinion that in order to draw the unchurched that more current pop styles should prevail, but no matter the music, let it point to and glorify the Living God.

As we desire to bring excellence from our music, let any attraction that may focus on those on the platform be reflected as forms of gratitude to God. This is one of the challenges we face as we build our churches, and the challenge is ultimately personal. The challenge to pursue excellence and to demand this focus is one that should be at the center of anyone who is on the platform or who serves in audio/visual or greeting. This challenge is the charge of the worship leader or pastor to counsel. But, as we are sure not to have worship center around a man or a woman, let that worship leader or pastor be in line with Proverbs 3:5-6 and be counseled by the senior pastor.

There is a section in this book for each component of Phase 1:

Excellence in Worship
Connecting in Worship
Worship Expressions
What to Bring to the Platform

## Phase 2 and 3 Overview

Phases 2 and 3 in establishing a worship culture are ways to help expand the reach of the Sunday (and/or other day of the week) experience. These phases are not necessary in order to build a culture of worship. Then why do them, you ask!? They are designed to enhance the worship experience as well as prepare the church for larger numbers.

There will be those church builders who will want to design these phases in from the beginning, and those who do not wish to do so at all. I don't think that Jesus tells us about either way, rather He tells us to worship in spirit and truth. There will be those church designers who will want to incorporate portions of Phases 2 and 3, but these phases rely heavily on Phase 1.

If a church doesn't concentrate on Phase 1, they will fail at Phases 2 and 3. Let us all make the decision to worship Him alone, regardless of our choices in building a church. *In Christ alone, I make my stand!*

## Phase 2: Color

God has provided astounding beauty in this world for us to behold and has given us the senses to appreciate His majestic creation. Psalm 19:1 states:

***The heavens declare the glory of God;***
 ***the skies proclaim the work of his hands.***

He intentionally created us so we significantly respond to beauty. Visual art touches us in unexplainable ways. Our souls are refreshed and moved. We have used art and stained glass and the interpretation of visions for centuries to vividly describe the wonders of God.

Phase 2 is engaging art and technology to help with the environmental worship experience. This includes lights, lyric, video and environmental projection. Again, removing distractions is the

## PHASE OVERVIEW

number 1 priority of us humans in our worship, so let us not add distractions as we add all of these lights and visual experiences. Rather, let us use technology to deliver excellence in our experience and all the while be conscious of the power to easily distract.

As we utilize technology, let it only enhance the worship experience and not become an idol. The design of Phase 2 technology could ultimately create a worship of the church building and experience itself, so a caution here to realize when it's time to reign in the monster and re-establish the worship priority.

Basic lighting can be done so tastefully. Let us allow God's creation of light and color to flourish in our services.

# Chapter 2:
# Phase 3: Community

## Phase 3: Community

Phase 3 is establishing an extended worship team or worship arts ministry. A church could include dance, art, drama, and poetry into the services. Or a church might give opportunities for their members to express themselves artistically by creating ministries or opportunities so members can contribute to an art gallery or the decoration of the sanctuary. The expression of song and of arts is a powerful worship tool for the good of the immediate community as well as to provide works of art for the larger church and local community.

The church seems to have had periods of time where it was the patron of artists and times that it didn't care so much for them. I contend that the beauty of God is found in our crafts, and the Bible is full of language describing the wonders of crafts and the skilled artisan. I contend that all of it is an expression of worship, whether or not the artisan believes that to be so!

So, wouldn't it follow that the artisan who follows Jesus and cares for excellence should be given a platform in the church? I'll leave you with that thought to ponder for your own local community.

The Expansion of the Music Ministry

The expansion of the music ministry of a church seems very natural to me, but of course, I am a musician! Never the less, I see just how strongly musicians can contribute to the welfare of the church body and how easily they can contribute to our worship services and other ministries.

A church might want to establish a larger music ministry to help minister to a larger need of worship services that happen within some of the ministries of the church.

You can think about establishing a worship choir as well as a songwriting ministry. This extension of worship arts helps to nurture the desires of those attending the church who feel that they want to give to the community as they have been gifted.

An example is Hillsong church of Sydney, Australia. Early on in their DNA, they designed to expand their worship music community by utilizing a choir, a band, and a network of songwriting musicians to nurture their nucleus. The results for them have been a stunning example of how a church can begin locally and touch hundreds of people in their community and then impact the lives of thousands of people all over the world.

**So, create an overall music ministry within your church.** When the worship band has been

## PHASE 3: COMMUNITY

established, hold auditions on regular intervals to plug singers and musicians into the larger music ministry. The church then advertises to the flock that there are musicians available to lead worship for their small group activities. What follows is a description of this larger music ministry with some of the areas where musicians can serve.

### Hold Regular Auditions

Rather than have auditions that are strictly for the worship band or for the choir, hold regular auditions for people so they can be plugged into your overall music ministry. Have an application form and video or mp3 auditions as well as live auditions and interviews.

Tell them of all the opportunities that are available and the view of the overall music ministry of the church. Always give them 'vision, vision, vision'.

Establish an online discussion forum for all involved in music for the church. As the administrator of the forum, begin discussions such as, "What songs would you like to hear at our church?" "How can we reach our larger community with music?" "What are your favorite songs and why?"

Hold the bar of excellence high. Begin assessing people with thoughts similar to the graph below.

*About the worship service graph below*: This graph is a rough sketch of an idea that speaks to two important areas of consideration, in my opinion, in regard to joining a worship team. One consideration for potential members is that of assessing the heart for worship. Another is that of assessing the musical

## LEAD WORSHIPERS

talent of the person. What I've done is to create a chart in the spirit of many psychological assessments where the upper-right quadrant is the 'ideal candidate'. The two categories, heart of worship and musical talent, aren't meant to correlate but are meant to give a visual on where you see a person.

Mark on this graph where you see the person in terms of musical skills and the heart for worship and make notes as to their future spiritual development needs. Make a plan to have a conversation with the lead or spiritual development pastor about the person.

For example, a person who approached you that is a great music talent and also has a wonderful personal relationship with God might be the 'perfect candidate', but maybe a person with a large music talent and no relationship or a person who is searching will give you the chance to consider whether or not that person would be ok to pursue. Maybe that person would be best as an alternate, or maybe you or your church decides that it is / is not ok for that person to be on the platform. The idea is for you to just make up a chart so you can begin assessing and begin having conversations. Make notes on this however it makes sense to you and your situation.

# PHASE 3: COMMUNITY

| | |
|---|---|
| Medium Heart of Worship<br>Medium Musical Talent | High Heart of Worship<br>High Musical Talent |
| Low Heart of Worship<br>Low Musical Talent | Little Heart of Worship<br>Little Musical Talent |

*Worship Service Graph*

    Allow people to become a part of your music ministry if you feel they can contribute toward the passion of worship. Have the mindset of the overall ministry. If you feel a person is a fit for a certain music ministry, fit them in and welcome them to the larger team and plug them in to the community discussion forum.

    If they belong in the overall music ministry, but you're not sure where they would fit, welcome them to the larger team and plug them in to the community discussion forum. If you don't feel they can help the church musically, give them specific items to work on and improve upon and invite them back to the audition next year.

    You're not going to please everyone, but don't turn away musicians and songwriters just because they're not a fit for the platform. Plug them in to the forums, the choir and to the songwriting ministry (see below for more on the choir and songwriting ministries).

## LEAD WORSHIPERS

Again, allow people to become a part of the music community as a whole as the first step. Then allow them to be called later to specific musical tasks, such as the worship team or as a solo music minister for a small group activity or to the choir.

We desire people who want to learn the ways of worship as it relates to being a musician in the church. We desire people who want to learn to praise God with their voice and instrument while being discipled in the ways of worship leadership.

We want to cultivate musicians who are hungry to worship and are hungry to learn about the removal of distractions from worship. This is a way to establish an artist roster for churches so they have fresh musicians and singers for multiple services. While it's definitely desirable for one cohesive band to play for all the services, there are times when this will be difficult.

The way this is handled will always vary from church to church, but the common thing is that musicians will leave. This gives the opportunity for new musicians to rise up within the community rather than seeking outside.

Have this network of musicians in constant communication. Have the concept of One Team, One Goal. Plug all of them into a common discussion forum to keep the ideas coming. Plug all members into planned nights of worship and into a songwriting community.

Establish Two Choirs

So many people love to sing. So many people want to help others worship. It's important to help create a great Sunday/other day worship experience by offering the choir experience. This is a time-immemorial western church practice that will

## PHASE 3: COMMUNITY

enhance any service. Some churches will decide that a choir only needs to be used for special occasions, some for every worship service. Either way, we owe this rich experience to both the singer and the congregation.

Whether you begin with a small number or a large number, do not overlook that each person auditioning needs to exhibit the same qualities as any musician on the platform.

I believe that churches might consider having two choirs: a worship choir and a larger choir.
Let's start small with the worship choir.

You could call these people background singers if you wanted. Establish a small number of singers that you can place on the platform, whether they are huddled around one or two microphones or whether they are on a riser. These people should be there because they WANT to lead worship. Raise the bar and expect excellence.

They become the face of the church just as anyone else on the platform becomes nakedly visible. I expand on this visibility in the section on *Connecting in Worship*.

These harmony and melody criers will bring much joy and passion to your service!

When you're ready, establish a large choir. Make passion of worship and musical excellence part of the criteria. Establish the importance of this culture in all that you do in your church.

Again, raise the bar and create a culture of excellence. Your auditions should have that wonderful balance of musical giftedness and the heart of worship.

# LEAD WORSHIPERS

<u>Establish a Songwriting Ministry</u>

There is a need to bolster the local and larger church communities with new songs which are theologically correct. Christian songwriters need to understand their role as true criers of the church and of the faith. They need to learn how to be gospel sharing leaders.

Some members of the worship band will be a wonderful fit in this group. Other non-musicians or musicians who may not aspire to Sunday worship might be interested as well. Have open mic nights and idea exchanges. Encourage the band members to help nurture songwriters of the congregation so their works can be introduced at nights of worship.

Among learning the ways of word crafting a lyric, there is a story telling function as well as a way of writing that engages the listener/worshiper. Some members will be lyric-only writers and will collaborate with musicians, some will write both music and lyrics. Learning to write engaging melodies is another challenge to grasp.

There will be songwriting exercises and workshops on items such as song legal concerns. This ministry can provide the local church with songs for worship, but most definitely provide the songwriter with worship songs for blessing others in their families and for other Followers.

This can also expand outside to bless others with good songs for their worship communities. Create the ability for songwriters of the church to join together. Offer classes and workshops to hone their craft. Make it possible for them to connect with each other and enrich our lives!

# PHASE 3: COMMUNITY

### Have Nights of Worship

Have the worship leader and band put together a night of worship every few Sundays or so. Have the worship band be expanded by guest musicians and singers in the church on these nights. Have this worship night be a place to have new songs of worship introduced that were written by the community.

People will be truly blessed that they have the opportunity to worship again at a church service that has a song heavy format.

### Offer Worship Music to Ministries

Announce to the church leaders that worship musicians will be available for their bible studies, small group activities or their own nights of worship. This is a great tool to create excitement about new worship songs and to extend the church family worship experience. Having musicians at some outreach events will also be very well received. Let the power of worship music help to take us to the throne room in our small gatherings!

## Summary of Phase 3: Community

Build a ministry of people who are passionate about delivering and teaching the ways of worship arts! Publish your vision and outline of the ministry. As you invite people and talk about the ministry, always give 'vision, vision, vision'. In discipling them along the way, always give 'vision, vision, vision'.

# Chapter 3:
# Excellence in Worship

## I Am So Very Fortunate

Since I can remember anything, the call on my life has been to give of myself musically in worship. I taught myself how to play guitar when I was twelve years old. I bought a book of chords and just began learning the shapes and how to coordinate that with a light strum. I was completely *hooked*. Hook, line, and sinker, that was me then and that is me now today. I began playing in church three weeks later with other young guitar players. That first year of playing was absolutely life changing, and I find no coincidence whatsoever that I gave my young heart to Christ that very same year.

*"Let the message of Christ dwell among you richly as you teach and admonish one another with all wisdom through psalms, hymns, and songs from the Spirit, singing to God with gratitude in your hearts."*

- **Colossians 3:16**

So, I am called to worship Him in song, but I am also called to let the message of Christ dwell in my heart. This passage from Colossians is one of many that talk about worshiping and learning more about God using singing as a tool. As such, this tool is only a portion of my calling. The experience of music will amplify the dwelling of the word of God in my heart! This is what a team of worshipers are called to express. The combination of song and God's word is beautifully powerful.

## We Are So Very Fortunate

We have all had similar calls from God, and we have been placed together for such a time as this. Together as one team, we have been called as individuals, as members of the body of Christ, to utilize our talents and our passions to create a harmonized worship. Whether you are a vocalist, musician, sound tech or a visual tech we come together to create that harmony for the good of our gathered people.

Individually, we search our hearts for the reasons that we are called. We work out our salvation using these gifts. We come as individuals, but together we are the body of Christ. **We come together to serve the body for our worship services and become a team.**

## Attitudes and Focus

What we do on the platform, or as a sound or visual tech, is on display for the entire congregation to see. This gives us a marvelous opportunity to become leaders of worship! We are the examples of excellence in worship in our community as well as examples of how our church views the importance of congregational worship. The pressure is on. Embrace this.

The difficult part is always going to be in our attitudes. The negative part of our attitudes is stuff that will always be hard to shake. 'Do I look good, do people think I'm worthy, oh I look so fake, I can't perform too well, is this worship or is this a show?!' Or we say, 'I suck! What am I doing up here? I really blew that last part!' The list of possibilities is long.

The positive part of our attitudes on the platform is NOT the polar opposite of the above, as the evil one would have you think. Rather, it is the removal of the negative! It is paving the way and preparing our minds to allow the Holy Spirit to use us.

**The idea is to effectively deal with all the negativity in our minds and remove it.**

'Selfish' covers the entire gamut of an overt attitude of 'look at me' as well as introverted thoughts of 'I don't like the way I look'. No matter where the thought falls on the scale, these thoughts are manifest in our expressions and draw attention to ourselves.

**Excellence in worship has everything to do with attitude and focus.** Focus on why we are here. The more we concentrate on the reasons why we are here, the more our selfish attitudes fade. This is a constant battle, not a one-time graduate school program.

# LEAD WORSHIPERS
## We Encourage Others to Worship

We must focus on the task at hand! The reason we are here and what we are presenting is SO important. What IS the task at hand? *We are here to make it possible for others to feel encouraged. People have had a tough week, or season in life and they come because Christ offers them rest. People come to sit and absorb, or they come ready to participate in worship.*

Let us pave the way for them and encourage them to participate in worship. Their hearts and minds are ready to give vocal thanks to the Almighty so let us not get in the way of that. And for those who come to sit and absorb, let us be an example that they can choose to stand and worship instead. Let us not give them any reason to focus on us.

*"Sing to him a new song; sing skillfully with a shout of joy"* – Psalm 33

Music is so powerful! We are the front line of the church, the face of worship at our church. People love to listen to skilled musicians all day long. King David hired 288 musicians and three leaders in 1 Chronicles:25 because he knew the importance of excellence. The music we put forth shows people just whether or not we as individuals care about the quality of our presentation to God. So, let us focus on contributing quality music as a team in order to present a fragrant offering to God. This attitude of ours will show.

The congregation needs to see from us that it's not only OK, but that it's a biblical and a very fulfilling time when we all participate in worship together.

## Removing Distractions

A part of our focus is to intentionally remove distractions. Distractions can be many things. Let each one of us identify some of these and pray for their removal. Above all, let's talk. Keep communication open with me as your lead worshiper about your struggles. Here's a short list:

- When I'm not good in my relationship with God
- When I'm not prepared musically
- When my head is buried in the music stand
- When I'm more concerned about how I look or perform
- If I look too 'lost in space' (see *Connecting in Worship*)

## We Must Raise the Bar

What we present to God is important. What we present to the body is important. It cannot be, 'oh, it's only church', 'why knock myself out or inconvenience myself'. Check it off my weekly to-do list. No, we must raise the bar of how we do worship at our church.

God deserves our excellence and not our table scraps! Now life is tough, I know. It's often hard to concentrate on all that life requires of us. But as long as we are in service of Him and our church on this front line, we will strive to be our best. And our best will show through.

We raise the bar in two areas: corporate worship and individual contribution. In corporate worship, we as a team are raising the bar and will show the people that we are excited and hungry to offer worship! We as a team really want to show that we are paving the way for others to be excited and will worship with us.

In raising the bar of individual contribution, we are called to improve our skills in our service to God. We are constantly managing curve balls thrown at us in life and are especially challenged along the path of self-improvement. We should look at those challenges as an opportunity for God to work within us. In our weakness, He is strong. In our struggles, He is glorified. It's certainly not the challenges and struggles that are glorified. The challenges and struggles are the lessons along the path of life which are tools that hone us and that will be used by God. Allow yourself the opportunity to grow your skills and to bring God more glory in the process.

These examples of raising the bar are wonderful ways of showing others that our callings are simply an act of life-long worship.

### We Live and Worship in God's Economy

As we lead others in worship, and as we show how we live our lives in an act of worship, we are an example to this church body of how God's economy works when He has gifted us.

In Matthew 25:14-29, we read a parable where Jesus tells us about God's economy in the kingdom of heaven. The master gives three servants three different amounts of money to guard while the master is away. The first is given the highest amount, the second a lesser amount, and the third a small amount. When the master returns, he finds that the first two servants that were given the larger amounts had invested the money and had returns on their investments. He tells them, 'Well done', and gives each an appropriate job according to their money management skills. The third servant was afraid of losing what was entrusted to him, and so hid the money.

When the master confronts the servant who hid the money, he asked him why he did so. "I was afraid of losing the money and I was afraid of you, master, so I hid the money so it would not be lost", the servant replied.

"Use it for excellence or lose it", the master replied! And that single bag of money that the servant returned was given to one of the servants who had invested wisely. The story is about our rewards and our responsibilities in the kingdom of heaven.

All the talents and treasures that we have, and don't have, belong to God, not us! How we
manage our money and talents for God determine how WE are blessed in this life and the next. We invest in our skills for our benefit as well as for the benefit of the body of Christ.

*"Without having seen the Sistine Chapel one can form no appreciable idea of what one man is capable of achieving."*

*-Johann Wolfgang Goethe*

> Always be willing to develop your musicianship and technical skills.

## The Call of Sacrifice

We are called to sacrifice in ministry. This can mean many things, and some of the particulars are going to be different from place of worship to place of worship. But there are a few that will be common. The overall level of sacrifice is going to depend on your agreement with your pastors. Here's a short list:

### Give 110%

Giving 110% means that when you're on the schedule, you're on for the commitment of preparing and worshiping to the full. Regular time off the schedule is planned, so you can concentrate on other life matters.

### Commitment to practice routines and rehearsals

Preparation of your part of the whole will need to be done on your own schedule. Rehearsals are when all the individual parts come together to form the whole. You will need to be committed to this process, whether you are a musician, vocalist, or lighting technician.

### Rearrangement of life in order to serve

# EXELLENCE IN WORSHIP

When you are on the schedule, things in life that can be made second place need to become second priorities. The call to serve should become the priority and treated with the importance it deserves.

## Getting a good night's sleep and taking care of your health

We need to take care of ourselves for a wide variety of reasons in life. If you are a person where much is required, much will be asked of you. Take care to get a good night sleep before honoring God, so He can have your full attention the next day.

## Prepare Spiritually

Spend time in preparation with the Word and in the presence of God before serving. Put on the armor of God as spoken of in Ephesians chapter 6. An excellent way is to also worship with the upcoming songs.

## Sacrifice some of your personal connection time during worship

For those in service on the platform, save some of your attention during worship to engage others with smiles and eye contact. Exhort those in the congregation to join you in worship. By all means, worship while you are on the platform and keep in mind the reason you've been called to be visible. For those who serve and are not visible, never once believe that you are not important because you are not visible. Always know and understand the crucial impact that environmental reinforcement (sound and lights) plays in providing an atmosphere of worship. You hold the power in determining how the musicians sound and you hold the key to providing and creating the right mood for worship.

## Got Jesus?

You will be asked if you have given a spoken commitment to Christ. I believe that any person on any leg of the journey to Christ should be offered a position. But I believe it's important that the person be open to growing in their relationship with God. The short answer must be:

> Yes, I am a follower of Jesus.

I know that this will not be the right answer for some churches, and really, that's ok. It's their call. I fully understand their desire to either hire musicians for ability or to allow musicians to serve that don't necessarily have a relationship with Jesus. That is completely ok.

*But my philosophy is this: when building a family of worshipers, the need to be a follower of Jesus is paramount when creating an atmosphere that desires to invite others to do the same!* I, or other pastors, must come along side others in the family and walk with them on the road to learning about Jesus. We must invest further in the challenge of discipleship. Ignoring this would be a huge disservice to the family. We should be hungry and become stronger together.

So, regardless of the criteria for joining service in church and the worship team, a question should be posed of each person on a regular basis:

# EXELLENCE IN WORSHIP

How is your walk with Jesus?

This needs to be done both in small group form as well as one-on-one pastoring. Let the methods of each be determined by each family.

---

<u>My Service Pledge</u>

By being a member of this team, I pledge to:
- Be on time
- Give 110% when I am on the schedule
- Practice my parts at home because rehearsal is where we come and put our parts together
- Come spiritually prepared
- Learn what it means to encourage participation and be distraction-free
- Pursue continuing education with my voice and/or instrument
- Be open about my walk with Jesus

# Chapter 4:
# Connecting in Worship

## Remove Distractions and Allow Others to Worship

Most people on Sunday morning are musically ignorant. I don't mean that in a negative way, what I mean is that people don't come to be critics of how you play the C chord or how the song is arranged or whether it's two- or three-part harmony. And we shouldn't expect them to discern these details or how smooth our transition was from song 3 to song 4.

What they want to do is to connect with God and to connect with the body. They want to experience the moments and emotions that bring them closer than ever to the Holy Spirit. They want to feel emotionally involved with God in a way that helps them relax and not be distracted by the trials of life.

Our job is to do our part and identify and remove the distractions we might present so we don't disturb that flow! We labor to identify and remove these distractions prior to Sunday so that on Sunday, all of our energy is placed into providing those connections.

In order to place our energies into connecting, it's important to place ourselves into the congregation's shoes and to understand why they come to church. All people come for three main reasons: to be captured and engaged, to experience moments and to be transformed. Even those who aren't ready to commit to God come for the same reasons, just on a lesser level.

## To Be Captured and Engaged

The vast majority of people come to church to be captured and engaged, to be swept up in the Holy Spirit. They want to be fed the nourishment of life through excellent spiritual music and the delivery of the Word. They want to be completely engrossed and caught up in each moment, and every eye and mind will be focused up front. And we who are called to serve in worship, musically and technically, are to provide a clear pathway for them to enjoy the fellowship of God and each other. Prepare the way of the Lord!

They want to see a confident stage full of charisma. What I don't mean is individual confidence to the point of cockiness and I don't mean the type of charisma found in jumping all over the stage. What I do mean is confidence in our abilities so we engage them and encourage them to worship and show them leadership in worshiping. *Let's not leave them on their own while we figure out what we're doing up there.* What I do mean is charisma that shows how captured those of us are also by the Holy Spirit as we smile and have good eye contact as we connect with them.

For those who come to church to kick the tires on Christianity, or who might not wish to engage, may our attitudes be infectious.

## To Experience Moments

People come to church to experience the healing grace of God. They come to experience those moments of connection with Him that speak into their lives. God willing, we are individual and collective conduits of that grace. Pray that we are a path for those who seek His face. We are there to help provide and nourish these moments for the people. People will want to come again and again to a place where they are free to work out their Sunday connection with God in an environment where their moments are cherished and nurtured by the worship and tech teams.

If you ask people, they may not be able to articulate that the reason they come to church is for these moments. They know that they want to come and sing worship songs in honor of God. Music is such a wonderful and unique conduit of communication between our heart, mind and souls and God. Great songwriters will continue to help us have these heart-felt moments of praise. Often, we can't explain why that happens. But as leaders of worship, our job is to identify those moments and sustain that momentum.

## To Be Transformed

People come to church to learn the ways of our new life in Christ. We come to be transformed by the renewal of our minds (Rom 12:1-2) and to see and feel how the richness of transformation is beneficial to our lives (John 10:10). *People come because they **want** to be transformed.* They come to hear the message from the songs and the teaching so they can be fed.

The message that the teaching team and the songs must give is that believing in God and believing on the promises of Jesus is a paradigm shift; a new way of living and thinking.

Our job as worship leaders is to set the table so this can happen. We can make it so we have an environment for people to come so they can be captured and engaged. We can make it so people are free to experience the moments of God's grace. And we pray that what we do paves the way for God to move as people work out their salvation.

The actual transformation is up to *God's* timing for the individual, but setting the table is up to *our* timing and our willingness to serve!

## Our Sacrifice

### Self-sacrifice of Our Personal Worship Time

We may be called to sacrifice our personal worship time. I wouldn't suggest that we are giving up all of our worship time, but some of your energies are going to be required in leading others. Save your best worship time for your quiet times during the week. This self-sacrifice is an attitude. The enemy of self-sacrifice is self-consciousness. When we're preoccupied with ourselves we have no time for this sacrifice. This is another huge reason to be musically prepared.

# CONNECTING IN WORSHIP

I know that while on the worship stage I naturally think of being full of worship and willing to help others participate. But the flesh that wars within me always tries to steal the show, and it is only through the grace of Christ that I am rescued (Rom 7:21-25).

We're all the same, up on the platform, in the tech booth or in the congregation. The problem is that we are the ones up there and have the attention of the people. Therefore, unless we make a conscious decision to 'outlaw' the flesh, it will rule us.

But here's the catch: I *am* going to fail. I am going to fail. The flesh wars within me against the Spirit of God that lives within me. So, I endeavor to set aside the war during my time of leading worship.

Together, we will do our best to not let the flesh win during this time. We still will fail and do and say funny things, for that is life. But we make the conscious effort to sacrifice SOME of our personal worship time and MOST of our spiritual warfare time in favor of having great eye contact and smiles. This is why it is imperative to come spiritually prepared, for the flaming arrows of doubt will be pointed at you.

How do we block this internal warfare for this time? We don't give the evil one a chance. Spiritual preparation, musical and technical readiness will allow our best to shine through. *Eye contact, smiles, and an attitude of giving until it hurts.* But here's the second part:

Don't let the false humility of the "lost in space" look (when you're praying but then you lose it or are attacked by negative thoughts) rule you. This can take you 'out of the zone'. People notice when you become distracted and look like you're praying when you're actually not!

# LEAD WORSHIPERS

Absolutely worship and revel in the Spirit of God! BUT we as leaders need to sacrifice some of our time doing so in favor of leading and connecting with the people and smiling.

<u>Personal Sacrifice of Time Used in Preparation</u>

You are giving a full-time commitment to the team. I don't mean that you are always available to play, sing, or run lights. What I mean is that when you are on, you are all on. A total of 110% for personal preparation (music/tech and spiritual) time, rehearsal time and worship time is required. You will be scheduled accordingly, depending on your individual needs and desires.

There is the preparation of music and your personal practice time during the week. Remember that when we get together to rehearse, we are putting our individual parts together. If you are not prepared, then WE are not prepared. Let us be strong together as one team!

I want to encourage you again to also spiritually prepare. Spend time praying with these songs and prepare by putting on the armor of God (Ephesians 6:10-18). Spend time with the Word of God and let it dwell in you richly (Col 3:16). Save your best worship for your personal quiet times. There is just no substitute for spending personal time with the Lord.

We offer our best effort of musicianship to Christ, to the team and to the body of the church without thought of personal glory.

Our sacrifice is in the preparation of our mind and body. Eat a good meal the evening before or at breakfast on Sunday morning and to plan to get a good night sleep.

# CONNECTING IN WORSHIP

Your preparation for worship should be that of an athlete preparing for the Olympic Games.

Excusing Yourself from the Team

Examine your heart from time to time and examine your commitment level. There could come a time when you are feeling overwhelmed by life or crushed by circumstances. You might have personal items that you need your attention. Or, you might find that there comes a time when the attitude just may not be right for worship or leadership.
If any of these reasons occur, consider asking to remove yourself from the team for a week or a short
season.

*Honestly, it's not about me being a judge of your character, it's about you recognizing the need to nurture and guard your heart.*

It's the need to strengthen your relationship with God. It's also about your giving level to the congregation and your willingness to put on your best attitude when on the platform.

Summary

Let me summarize on our personal sacrifice on the platform: It's all about the *proactive* giving of your best effort to God and to the people and to be willing to wash their feet (John 13:13-15). It is NOT about being *reactive* to the previous list of 'rules' I just wrote. It's *not at all* about concentrating on 'what not to do', rather, it's all about preparation and giving.

With the proactive attitude of giving, all of our efforts will align as they should.

Understanding the call to leadership on the music and tech teams is similar to understanding Paul's letter to people about the basics of Christianity: It's all about Jesus and what He did for us, not Jesus plus any list of rules (Galatians 5:1, 6).

Yes, we are holding ourselves to a higher standard than the rest of the congregation, but we have placed ourselves in the position of high vision. Let us not shrink from this position and be self-conscious, but instead let us perform our duty in pointing the people to the cross of Jesus.

## Leadership in Worship

Here's why you are a worship leader: You are up there and a face of the church. Not only do you have the responsibilities I just described, but also any person might approach you. You need to have the attitude of leadership in order to answer people's questions. This is not about you having all the answers. It's about you being ready to listen and to give the proper advice. Listening and talking with people is one thing, but you also need to be aware of how to connect a person with the right leader or other person for information or counsel. You need to be prepared with a basic knowledge of church ministries and who is in church leadership roles.

A person may approach you for prayer. Please do pray with them, but if you don't have time or are not comfortable doing that, connect them with a prayer team person or a leader of the church.

# Chapter 5:
# Worship Expressions

## Cool Lights! What's Missing??

Cool lights, awesome background, nice message, great songs ... What's missing?? Number one: remember to open yourself to the Holy Spirit. What else? Read below.

## Bring it On

You're in the congregation and you see the guitar player all meek and nervous and head buried. You start praying for him or her, right?? You don't understand music theory or guitar, but you do understand human behavior. Well, REALLY, what is one of the reasons you are praying? For you to quit feeling nervous for the guitar player! When you're sitting or standing in the congregation, you're in receive mode, right? You say, 'bring it on!!' You didn't come to witness a nervous guitar player and you just missed a great lyrical passage.

How can we 'bring it on' if all we show is nervousness? We can have the slickest motion graphics, the most awesome band, but if we don't have LOVE, we are nothing but a clanging bell and a noisy gong! Where's the love? We need to bring confidence and authority to the platform. Not cockiness, arrogance and false humility. No! We need to bring the confidence and authority to be the messengers of God's love on the platform. The people EXPECT us to bring it on! So, bring it! Be authentic, be prepared. Understand your roles and engage the congregation. Free them up to worship to the full.

We need to create fine china moments for people to worship. No paper plates. God deserves our best intentions, not our afterthoughts. How very selfish of us to not bring our best.

Preparation to Serve Fine China Moments

We have our roles in preparation. Some choose the songs; others arrange them and others plan the service. Musicians need to do their planning by always being ready for the call to offer worship. Don't wait for the call that you will be playing in two Sundays and then begin preparing a week and a half later. Come completely prepared and ready to offer your best. Now you are bringing the fine china. Set the bar high for yourself.

Share Musical Moments

As a worship artist, we have been infused with ability that we MUST share. All of us spend many months or years trying to figure out what that means for our lives. We have been infused, commissioned by God to be used by Him. Not just the music part of us, but the artist part of us as well.

Learn to create those moments which allow the Spirit to move during worship. For example, we need to provide musical and vocal phrases where the congregation will respond. When these can be identified, band leadership should think about stretching that part for extra set of measures. This is sharing your God-infused, quality, DNA with the people. There are many aspects of this for us to explore. Search your hearts and consult your leaders.

<u>Team Dynamics</u>

Dual meaning: Musical dynamics as well as musical family dynamics. First, let's talk about musical dynamics.

The challenge we have as worship musicians is to present familiar or not-so-familiar songs each week. Often, we learn by getting the chord charts, lead sheets and mp3s of the radio version of songs. This sometimes works well for worship music, as many of them are recorded with thoughts of congregations or actually recorded before a congregation. But not all songs will be that way and will require some musical arrangement. Regardless if it's a well-known radio song, a new song or an older song without a reference recording, our challenge is to recognize and create dynamic swings within the song.

For example, we start soft and end huge, we start with keys only for the first, and then we add guitar and bass at the first chorus, or we begin singing softly and end singing with a fuller voice. These are only examples. Each song is the script and will tell you. Each song will present moments that will tell you what needs to be done.

A part of what I mean is this: to go about simply following notation or chord charts without building and utilizing musical dynamics, without the infusion of our individual and collective musicianship, is to short-change the worship experience. The leader is going to help mold these musical moments and may write these arrangements, but the individual musician must be aware of creating dynamics and bring their musicianship and suggestions to the table.

Here's one of our other challenges: musical family dynamics. We need to understand how each of us interacts with the other as it relates to our collective musicianship and 'bringing' worship. All people feed on relationships! We feed each other and we feed the congregation. The congregation wants to be involved in our platform relationships as well as for us to INVITE them into our relationships, ultimately inviting them into a relationship with God.

Expressions Summary

Ok, this is NOT about pushing the issue of 'moments' so hard that they are false or it becomes a show. Let us lean on the understanding of God while being an artist in service of Him. Know that the Almighty has placed the kernel of worship expression in you. The Almighty expects that you not ignore this. Share the gift of music and artistry, summoning confidence, and leadership with the people.

# Chapter 6:
# What to Bring to the Platform

For all of the talk about preparation and all of the talk about understanding what the congregation expects, the most important thing remains: bring joy and be open to the work of the Holy Spirit! Bring your passion for worship. We can get all of the technical right, but we will be a clanging gong without the most important reason we are there: to worship in spirit and in truth. And it is our job as worship leaders to 'bring it' and to worship. The Father wants our unity, and we need our unity of purpose in order to function as a people that God has ordained.

Extravagant Worship

Darlene Zschech of Hillsong Church of Sydney puts it this way: *we need extravagant worshipers on the platform*. Our attitude needs to be of joy and of service to others when we're scheduled. This is another reason why I've stated '110% when you're on the schedule'. We need worshipers who are not afraid to show their relationship with Christ and who are not afraid to lead others to the throne. We need parking lot attendants who will stand in the pouring rain in order to help a person into church.

> Have the attitude of Christ in Matthew 5 when he states in verse 41, "If a person forces you to go one mile, go with them two miles." Have the attitude of Christ when He washed the feet of His disciples.
>
> *"So he got up from the meal, took off his outer clothing, and wrapped a towel around his waist. After that, he poured water into a basin and began to wash his disciples' feet, drying them with the towel that was wrapped around him."*
>
> - John 13:4-5

Do what it takes to serve the people. Don't just tell/play/sing/produce for them, show them.

<u>Bring Joy</u>

Your passionate worship experience and your relationship with God are required. It is what the congregation wants to see. I'm not saying that everyone in the congregation wants emotional worship, what I'm saying is that everyone in the congregation needs to feel the freedom to express themselves in worship, no matter the expression. We are the leaders in providing that atmosphere! The joy

## WHAT TO BRING TO THE PLATFORM

that you feel and the happiness you have about Christ in your life should be on display for all to see.

Have a willingness to raise your hands and raise your face to heaven, or simply surrender yourself in worship. Again, I am not talking about over-emotional worship. I'm talking about worship where you are willing to lead others in approaching the throne. A closed countenance, which will be written all over your face, tells others that they're on their own for worship.

### Fuel, Fire, Furnace and Heat

John Piper uses this analogy that I want to share with you:

> The *fuel* of worship is the grand truth of a gracious and sovereign God; the *fire* that makes the fuel burn white hot is the quickening of the Holy Spirit; the *furnace* made alive and warm by the flame of truth is our renewed spirit; and the resulting *heat* of our affections is worship, pushing its way out in tears, confessions, prayers, praises, acclamations, lifting of hands, bowing low, and obedient lives.

As worship leaders, we want to bring the *fuel* of the grand truth to the congregation through skilled lyric and music writers. We amplify this truth and we *add kindling* with an excellent musical arrangement and lighting/visual presentations. We invite the Holy Spirit to be our worship leader and constantly pray for His quickening (the infusion of the Holy Spirit into our lives and the infusion of the Holy Spirit in leading our worship). *This quickening ignites the fire,* to make our worship white hot; our spirits are renewed.

The resulting heat of our expressions of worship, in the lifting of hands and the crying out to Him in petition, is *our cry of unity in purpose to the Father!!* Hebrews 10:25 tells us:

> *And let us consider one another in order to stir up love and good works,* ***not forsaking the assembling of ourselves together, as is the manner of some, but exhorting one another, and so much the more as you see the Day approaching.***

So let us as worship leaders always be of an inviting and serving nature. Let us all learn to be extravagant worshipers.

## Summary of Connecting in Worship

We plan so many plans and dream of worship services to have smooth transitions and great songs. There are Sundays that come and we're so proud of us and our song planning and of our sacrifice to set the table. And then worship doesn't go well! Then there are those Sundays where it felt like we 'winged it' for whatever reason, and it seemed like the Holy Spirit was there and took over the service! In a past church where I sang and played, we would call it the 'God Screen'. "The God Screen must have been up today, that's all I can say!"

We DO want to do our best to prepare and to understand and serve people in worship. We want to be conscious of how we connect with people and that we are bringing our best to God, but God will have His way with the service. If we are faithful to invite the Holy Spirit, and we bring our faith to the table we are

## WHAT TO BRING TO THE PLATFORM

setting for others, that is all we have, and the Holy Spirit will do the rest.

Let us pray that during our time of worship that all of us, platform, tech and congregation, are transformed
by the quickening of the Spirit so that the flame of praise rises high into the night to our God. Let us pray that all of us who have been called to play and sing and run lights and lead others for this time of worship are caught up with the Spirit in order to provide a sacred space for all of the family to know and feel just how much they are loved by the Creator of the Universe.

# Take the step to become an extravagant worshiper!!

****

## About the Author

Steve Cass has been playing and singing in church since he was 12 years old. He taught himself how to play guitar and has never looked back. A full- and part-time musician since 1970, Steve has been a member of church worship teams, advisory, and elder boards. He planted Bridge Covenant Church of Gilbert, AZ as worship leader. He's currently worship leader at Sunrise Church of the East Valley in Gilbert. He lives in Gilbert with his wife, Lisa.

Stephen Robert Cass has over 60 song titles listed at ccli.com and has produced 14 album projects.

Contact the author and copyright holder at steve@songs4god.net for bulk purchase discounts for both print and eBook.

Please leave an honest and simple review at Amazon, or your favorite book place. Thanks!

# LEAD WORSHIPERS

## Titles by Stephen Robert Cass

### Fishing in Church: How to Be a Congregational Songwriter
*A blueprint for learning the craft of congregational songwriting and getting your songs heard*

### The 5 Steps to Get Your Songs Heard
*A Congregational Songwriting Plan*

### The 5 Keys to a Clear Mix: Create YOUR Mix Philosophy
*for Christian Artists, Songwriters, and Church Song Mixers*

### Worship Songs and the Law: How Churches Stay Legal and How Songwriters Get Paid
*Honor God and Honor Songwriters*

### The Harmony for Worship Project
*Training Voices to Praise the Living God*

### The Proverbs 27.17 Song Critique Method
*The Power of Group Learning to Deliver Songs*

www.ingramcontent.com/pod-product-compliance
Lightning Source LLC
Chambersburg PA
CBHW070338120526
44590CB00017B/2934